Island on the Wind-Breathed
Edge of the Sea

Island on the Wind-Breathed
Edge of the Sea

John B. Lee

First Edition

Hidden Brook Press
www.HiddenBrookPress.com
writers@HiddenBrookPress.com

Copyright © 2011 Book – Hidden Brook Press
Copyright © 2011 Poetry – John B. Lee

All rights for poems revert to the author. All rights for book, layout and design remain with Hidden Brook Press. No part of this book may be reproduced except by a reviewer who may quote brief passages in a review. The use of any part of this publication reproduced, transmitted in any form or by any means, electronic, mechanical, photocopied, recorded or otherwise stored in a retrieval system without prior written consent of the publisher is an infringement of the copyright law.

Island on the Wind-Breathed Edge of the Sea
by John B. Lee

Layout and Design – Richard M. Grove
Cover Design – Richard M. Grove
Cover Photograph – Richard M. Grove

Printed and bound in USA

Library and Archives Canada Cataloguing in Publication

Lee, John B., 1951
    Island on the wind-breathed edge of the sea / John B. Lee

Poems.
ISBN – 978-1-897475-19-5

    1. Cuba--Poetry. I. Title.

PS8573.E38186 2008   C811'.54   C2008-907316-9

para mi amigo
Manuel de Jesus Velázquez León

Acknowledgments

Poems from Island on the Wind-Breathed Edge of the Sea have appeared in The Ambassador, Descant, Matrix Magazine and in my book, Never Hand Me Anything If I am Walking or Standing (Black Moss Press, 1994) That series of poems reappears herein with permission from Black Moss Press.

*a series of poems under the working title, Cuban Journey, won Matrix Magazine's Travel Writing Award.

Table of Contents

Preface — Island on the Wind-Breathed Edge of the Sea – *p. x*

Cuban Journey — the starving year

– Playing Tennis in Cuba – *p. 1*
– In the School Rooms of Cuba – *p. 2*
– There Are Twisters on the Northern Beaches – *p. 4*
– To Drink the Earth on the Far Shore with Thirsty Feet – *p. 7*

A Year of Drought — 2006

– Sealing the Jar – *p. 11*
– Remembering the October Missile Crisis
      with Cuban Friends – *p. 14*
– The Waters That Circle Us All – *p. 16*
– el mismo, la meme chose, the same – *p. 18*
– Charo de Maita – *p. 20*
– Flowers of Fire – *p. 22*
– The Drought – *p. 23*

Bad Water — 2007

– Bad Water – *p. 27*
– Astonished – *p. 29*
– The Lonesome Lovebird – *p. 32*

This Hand — 2008

– Hotel Tropicoco – *p. 35*
– The Mirrors of Eden – *p. 36*
– Listening – *p. 38*
– Hemingway's Mirror – *p. 39*
– There is a Story – *p. 41*
– This Is How I Know I Love You—a Cuban Valentine – *p. 43*
– The Informer – *p. 46*
– The Wind is Like a Thief – *p. 48*
– Mistakes Along the Way – *p. 50*
– The Lost Girl – *p. 53*
– This is What I Know of God – *p. 56*
– The Coat Within the Man – *p. 57*
– Real Shoes – *p. 58*
– This Hand – *p. 61*

Notes on the poems – *p. 62*
Biographical Sketch of Author – *p. 64*

Island on the Wind-Breathed Edge of the Sea ...

In the winter of 1992, my family and I flew to Santiago de Cuba and traveled from there by bus in the dark hours of a Caribbean night to our final destination at Marea del Portillo, a resort near the remote rural mountain community of Manzanillo. That year we woke to the sound of lean sows rooting the beaches, crossed paths with free-range roosters strutting the jungle trails and discovered tame horses grazing the hills. We feasted on fish and pork with the strong scent of guava wafting up from supper tables heavy laden with ripe fruit. We drank cold beer and sipped iced mango by the pool. Every morning we were greeted by pyramids of hard-boiled eggs and rashers of Cuban bacon. It wasn't until many years later that we learned how hard things were for the Cuban people after the collapse of the Soviet Union. We were told that, during what became known as "the starving year", every Cuban citizen lost on average twenty pounds due to a combination of galloping inflation and an overall shortage of essential resources.

Since that first visit, I have had the privilege and pleasure of returning to Cuba on three subsequent occasions. On each ensuing journey the conditions of the island have been much improved. In 2006 my wife and I journeyed to a resort near Guardalavaca, close to Cuba's second-largest city, Holguin. Then in 2007 and again in 2008, we stayed at Hotel Tropicoco, a Russian-built resort located twenty minutes by bus from the capital city of Havana. On all three occasions we traveled as a small delegation of authors representing a Canadian contingent of the 'Canada-Cuba Literary Alliance,' an international organization founded by Richard (Tai) Grove and his Cuban friend, language-professor/ translator/ author Manuel Velázquez León.

Little wonder then that the muses of Cuba have inspired my work. On the occasion of the first visit, I wrote a series of poems included herein under the title 'Cuban Journey.' This set of poems, first published in Matrix magazine, and published again in my book, *Never Hand Me Anything If I Am Walking or Standing*, won *Matrix Magazine's* 'Travel Writing Award,' in 1994.

Each return has resulted in writing. The year my wife and I lodged near Guardalavaca, we met professor Manuel Velazquez Leon, who translated several of my poems into Spanish. Bilingual versions were featured in an issue of CCLA's journal, *The Ambassador*. On that visit I read poetry in English and Spanish in a courtyard in Holguin along with fellow-Canadians Tai Grove and Ken Mitchell and three Cuban poets. That magical late-afternoon reading followed by dinner at an authentic Cuban restaurant remains an apotheosis of sorts for me as a poet.

In 2007, and then again in 2008, we stayed near Havana and made excursions into the city to read poetry, tour, and break bread with Cuban authors. Our first visit to the Canadian embassy included an hour-long chat with the ambassador. We also participated as readers in the Latin-American Book Fair at the old fort across the bay from the city. In 2008 we returned to the book fair, read again at the university and the main library, where a highlight of our reading tour involved an audience of grade one students visiting the library as part of their literacy training.

I hope to return to Cuba again to visit my friends and fellow-writers, and to partake of the generous and open-hearted hospitality of a people whose love for poetry and music is an example to the world.

Cuban Journey—the Starving Year—1992

Playing Tennis in Cuba

One cloud drifts by
like a puff of tractor fume
pausing over the long blue look of an armed guard
sitting by pups
near a hut
beside the tourist courts.
The dogs crawl about
at his feet
and thump their crooked tails
like fly whips in the dirt
while we play tennis
one man, one woman, one girl
and two boys tossing around
in the soft racket of the game
where the net hangs between posts
like a fisherman's ragged skein
not quite catching the weft of Caribbean wind
as a slip of tiny fishes
might school about and mock a place
too torn to mend.
And the pups yap importantly
like university poets discussing revolution over coffee
and watch us
lob against love.

In the School Rooms of Cuba

In the small closed schoolroom of Cuba
there are no books
and all the boys
bereft of pencil stubs have run outdoors
to bat their balls beyond the barbs
among the pigs and cactus.
And the slender brown-limbed girls
with almond eyes
jump laughing in the heat, their red skirts
flying
like the skip of wind and light
among the flowers
taking turns at the play of shadows
while on the dark slate inside
and in the musty texts the teachers use
there is a telling chalked
a story inked
about the days before the birth of beauty
when the mountains
crawled with guns and a peasant army scuttled
among the coconut crabs and goat dung
to cross the silting streams
wandering down to wet their snouts in the sea
while I stand and watch wishing I didn't
feel so much the careful-grammared school inspector
running his finger along a ledge
to see if it comes away yellow.

I wish I weren't such
a well-shoed stranger
thinking of home and my heritage
filling history scribblers
with celebrated rumours of a world
owned by all the wrong people.

There are Twisters on the Northern Beaches

Winds winding like spun sugar
coming down the sky
out of the hills
moving along the northern beaches
twisting through the royal palms
leaving an obvious trail of ruin
like spies going through suspicious rooms
so you could die if you wished it or not even on holiday
in the meningitis heat
of Cuba
and on the dirty little cactus trails
in among the coconut scraps
where large black beetles
lay siege tanking over goat dung
and pig spoor
while machete-wielding peasants
play their luck
against poison spiders
scuttling like scorched hands in the seared blight of dying trees
and the blood-stream springs
working the heavy rains
out of the soil
boiling down the pebble paths
for the brown edges of the coffee-coloured bay
soupy with silt
from the bland chemical erosion
of the loosening earth
or standing on the high cliffs
above the blue sea
among the dull-witted horses

taking the donkey marks up among the thorns
and grazing on spurs of dry grass
their ribs showing
like cedar ribs of rotten canvas boats
and look, see there, how the ground might give
on the precipice
and calve into air
a large assumption of itself
breaking off and sending your son
whaling down the sky
the stones shaling after
and fluking at his feet

or watch him gone in a scrambling descent
quickening in screed come loose
and marbling under his feet
like a slapstick scene
marbling Chaplin into the next room

or walking barefoot
in the still shallow pools
and stepping on a bitter slug
osmotic with poison
so you limp like a burr-pawed dog
and carry your shoes an hour
into the rusty construction site
spiked with careless carpenter traps
for the hapless Canadian fakir
who comes away shod like a tender-hoofed horse
with a two-nailed stud

and this is as far as you go
your life burned through in the middle
like the fiery smear
of a projection lamp too hot for the film
and three generations later
your great-great-grandnephews might speak of you
as the one who died
mysteriously young in Regina
leaving no clue to read
in your brother's memory
or the one who slipped away
into oblivion
on a swamp-mist morning
on a forgotten afternoon
your sister's children's children wondering who you were
or the one
who died on vacation
a thousand miles away
a Caribbean wind
carrying your name
like room service.

To Drink the Earth
on the Far Shore with Thirsty Feet

In the guava smell of Cuban hills
where peasant children walk barefoot among the pigs
truffling black-sand sows with bones
like old machines
abandoned in our nettle yards
and horses standing side by side with sway-back mules
wending their way
under a few glue-colourd clouds
and goats so lean they seem
to bleat
from leather cut and hanging draped across a crooked fence
and sheepos
carrying rags of wool by the tall palms
to taggle the wires where they pass
and Chanticleers sleek-feathered and proud-coxed
in the brood-light heat of a Caribbean sun
while child-small women
with such beauty in their faces
they seem the very soul of beauty
smiling
come and offer greeting
with tiny gentle hands
to touch our hearts
like bright fat birds
breathing in pet-shop cages after dark
while the blue sea rolls
in a dream-sleep wind
and we sit

in their houses
taking sweet strong coffee in dainty cups
and one drinking glass
in the half-light of a closed room
los ninos slap stepping
a low table
and keeping their distance
to love us for strangers
and palm the wood
to keep with the drunken balance
of learning to walk.

And there from that village
and from the charm of human hope
we return to the river
and cross where there is no bridge
feeling the water rise and run
to touch our ankles with cooling circles
then pausing to drink the earth on the far shore
with thirsty feet
we almost learn to remember the meaning of life.

A Year of Drought — 2006

Sealing the Jar

I see them floating
like ownerless ivory
these white bones of lost children
suspended in liquid
in the city museum of Holguin
the half-dozen un-nameable
pickle jars
of unborn daughters
and unblessed sons
and I am here
with the slow
amniocentesis of my soul
considering six
unknown and unknowable mothers
six anonymous fathers
also the final sad sigh
of the elders
sorrowing at the twice-crossed threshold
of life
the flesh font of women
the ripening womb
the ecstasy of conception
like the clairvoyant
apotheosis of a breaking fever
they cry out
like waterbirds

on a beach of dreams
that falling into darkness of song
an uncoupling
and parting the twin shades
of imagine and remember
with a faith and wisdom
surrendered to both directions
we enter
the blue beauty
of the undershell of heaven
and fly beyond the explosion of stars

old sentimentalist
of that second silence
but what of the first
I wonder
the before-life
just as the litmus of lovers
transforms
in the lip of the womb
like the dawn and the dusk
in the hour of oceans
at the crimson commence and the crimson regret

and so
of these shell-skulled
children
set in a row
like a lost tea service
of the wealthy dead

with the translucency
of sand dollars
thinned by the tide's small femurs
like struts of bottle boats
I wonder
who wept
at your crowning
who mourned
as you fell from regret
and who among angels
might curse us
for sealing the jar.

Remembering the October Missile Crisis with Cuban Friends, March 17, 2006

we were all merely children
scorched in the burnshadow
of thermonuclear war
as we crouched in crawl shades
at school
like sundials in gardens of noon
turned to salt
in the suddenly lucid illusions of light
and this was our lot
to live
among liars
while missiles bristled like coral in Cuba
and madness built shelters at home
stocked cupboards with cans and stale crackers
and we watched the grey box
in the parlour
for comforting tinctures of truth

and why were we slaves of such fires
ask the man with the hammering shoe
ask the handsome Narcissus
with his face an eventual coin
a profile in silver
like all ancient Caesars of Rome

ask Manuel
whose mother was frightened
by droning of bombers come low
and buzzing the fields near Holguin

I think now of dragon-flies
skimming their blue-green wet-winged reflections
in the gravel ponds of home
for now, we meet as friends
as gentle poets
of our own peculiar pasts

I can see
grim Grominko
I can see
Fidel
I can see
Kruschov, Kennedy
MacNamara
all those powerfully powerless men
who left us
children quivering in our feckless bodies
our fathers blanched and helpless
our teachers
rigid and stoic with instructions
as Ontario autumns rattled orange
and smouldering with deciduous doom.

The Waters That Circle Us All

the sunlight
on the Cuban coast
comes tinting the waters
like an indecisive overpainter
everchanging and tainting
the mutable hues of the sea
close by
the pale white sand shallows
are but a sallow green
a faded acquamarine
of ankle-stained statues
and almost chilly children
thrilled to be belly dry
and then the surface
is blackened by weed
like the ink shadow of clouds
locked in time, a vegetative blot
in the turquoise brilliance
the shiny undulations
lie shattered by foam-frilling white
like the ruff-collar throats
of gentlemen sailors arriving from Spain
Diego drowning
and the deep-water death of a king

what commingles here
among reefs
and shell shelves
where the seen combers shatter their will
is ocean enough

the swimmers, the
waders, the walkers
the watchers
the boaters, the
sailors
the waters that circle us all.

el mismo, la meme chose, the same

last night
the moon was shining
like a sugar bowl
and we set
the clock
in the ship of bones
by the pendulous tempo
of a garden swing
timed to the slowing of hearts at rest
in the heat
while the yellow sun plunged in the sea
with heaven dimming down
like a fever room
lost as we were in the great search
of the soul for the soul
like a fold on a fold
in old lace
and this is how it was
to see the Carilinda flowers
fallen like shedding of garments for bed
pink-feather blossoms
ballerina-frail costumes fashioned
for the customs of a gentle wind

this afternoon
we'd seen how the ox steer
pulled his yolk and cart
a pace   a pace
under avacado groves
mango, papaya
banana and the four-wife cart-driver
rattled his chain
so his thin horse 'el puma'
quickened his step
for the only living he knows
the culture of dung
on stone fields
and rough roads.

Charro de Maita

in this five-hundred-year-old burial grounds
of Charro de Maita, Cuba
the disinterred
bones of the past
lie about locked in sad grains of grim earth
as if assuming the multifarious postures
of bodies on beaches
what remains of the lost
the shipwrecked in time
their ribs like bent strakes of broken boats
their skulls
set deep in sorrows of sand
the knobs of their spines
have gambolled in traces
like the dullness of come loose stones
abandoned in games of metaphysical chance
'what are we'
they are saying
one jaw lapsed into laughter
one clenched on secret incisors of silence
some lie as if in utero
wombed in earth unborn
some lie
full stretched, arms crossed in grace of graves
like the breath of the vanishing heart
and the final sighing of faith

one is sternum down turned
with his breast to the ground
so his soul
will be smothered
like smoke by a rag in a hole
his to suffer the eternal malediction of the damned

what was his crime, I wonder
though I do not know
I dare not ask

and with these fifty-five indigenous dead
a single Spaniard
lies like an old-world graft in the new
among the loved by others
he tells his story
to the soil
in words of wind
and the language
of the living voices of the sea.

Flowers of Fire

the Spaniards came shining from waters
shining with swords and helmets
and breastplates shining
like Sunday silver
rattling courtesy in the rag sails
of great ships
looking for gold
and I am on
the northern beach
near Rio de Oro in Cuba
considering the statue of Columbus
his hat like a flat bread
his left hand
wounded by weather
like any other blackened crag
of the sea-washed coast
he is loosening his grip
in the stronger urgencies of time
and salt winds

he brought fear
to fishermen
silence to songbirds
from faraway failures of beauty
come close
with the Queen's acquisitive touch
her fingers like drought on the fronds
blight on the leaves
and the blunderbus flowers of fire.

The Drought

in the all inclusive
we stand laving ourselves
in the showers of the hotel
as if in an April rain
we lounge on the lovely beaches
of Guardalavaca
in the province of Holguin, later
we wade
waist deep in clear blue
walking cool bellied
for drinks at the pool bar
wait beside five or six
half-full abandoned glasses
Pina Colada, flat beer warming
in the sun, melting ices of mango
and strawberry
the sweet aromas of cocoa butter
shining from shoulders

and this in the season of drought
a year of no rain
with the fields burned brown
the palm fronds
dry and dropping
like the fan shadows that fall from sleepy hands
in Sunday gardens
and on the farms

the oxen walk
in drags of dust
and Manuel tells us
his father's sheep are dying of thirst
as we sip and lament
the close-at-hand grasses
and winter-faded flora go dim
in the cooling of heat

I see where the furrows have heaved
to the plough
like harbours in the wind
and thirsty horses graze the desiccated hills
and one farmer gathers fodder
stuffs his cart
like mattress ticking
taken home for feed

and we
are splashing
watching the work-maids
wash the walkways
knowing most tourists drink all day
till they're drunk
run taps for showering
flush the toilets twice
toss half-filled bottles in the trash
because the water's warm

watch the rainless heavens
grateful for
the cloudless blue

while someone's father's lambs
are falling
enfeebled in the pasture
their dam's teats dry
as gloves.

Bad Water — 2007

Bad Water

Agua malo in Spanish
they are bad water
beautiful blue manubrium
these ancient creatures
with toxic tentacles
floating in the currents of the Caribbean
drifting without locomotion
they follow the will of the wind
and the way of the tide
come shipwrecked to shore
in foolish and doomed
armadas of purple-spined sails
and translucent aquamarine and luminously lovely
fuchsias lashing the surf
with their sting
so swimmers burn in tangled strings of pain
and drown like sailors
with salt in the lash of their wounds

I and my little Portuguese event
was nettled
in the turning and turbulent
occurrence of a toenail-laving stroll
at the crest and release
of the last unlasting energy
of a single occupied wave
this gorgeous balloon
playing 'pay attention' in the beachwash
seared me arch and ankle
left and right
and like a sudden fire from war

in the twin-blood courses
of our self-inhabiting hearts
we met and gave
a greeting brief as death of joy

what consciousness
there was in membranous light
I saw
where it tumbled
and was moon-worthy
in the morning
sun-poor at noon
and dead by dinner
supper for the crabs

this man-of-war
like any storm-sought hero
of a stranger's ink
any one-armed admiral
of another age
sung loud in languages
we neither speak nor read
any much-hung portrait
of importantly fallen walls
any cutthroat pirate
and his secret casks of faded gold
any unspent and unspendable
thief of time
he turns his absence
in the mind of God
becoming the darkened sea
that holds him like a vanishing pool of light

Astonished

there is a poster on a billboard
above the sand-swept sidewalk
of a beach-street shop
in a local lake town
it shows a model in a bathing suit
and she is swimming in self seduction
the rayon ravishment of her private desire
revealed as a slight relief in the trace of a fold
like the manifest ripeness of plum
and her elbows are out
like half-folded wings of a waterfowl
coming to rest
and her thighs are flung wide as a bible
and her palms prove the femoral ardor of 'still'
like framing the frailty
with a carnal caress
and her eyes
flicker with feeling
as if they were fluttering shut
on the darkness of dream

and this is so matter of fact
among comers and goers
the hanger-rattling women and girls

who fling about
these flimsy silks
these flowering fabrics

draping their arms in the strap lines
and leg loops
like the fragrance of sleep on the floor

and as I think
on this week at the poolside
in Cuba
with no two swimsuits the same
how the girls
touched their toes
to the water
as if they were testing a bath
how they waded
in trails of reflection
how they dazzled the surface
with the slow irrumation
of undulous mirrors
unnatural blue
and some were drifting
like April in orchards
with the easy release of frail white
too weak to cling to the sky

and oh, the aromas of heaven
the vernal perfumes
of wet spring
with the sweeping of limbs into sweetness
like songbirds leaping the branch

and I am a muse
of such mystery

not by the brutal dogs of the law
will I be dissuaded
from beauty

not by the yawping of harpies
not by the lying of lawyers
for
we are
as it is with the fountainhead
of all creation
a complexity
in the quivers of Cupid

and I am
I assure you
a fletcher of fidelity

The Lonesome Lovebird

this is what it is
to be the lonesome lovebird
locked alone in a lobby cage in Cuba
fluttering like the swirl of waved-away smoke
with a crimson bill
like the lipstick rub
of a lost kiss let drift
the widow, the orphan, the fat child
the bachelor, the elder, the ill
the out-too-far
caught in the slipstream
caught in the storm
being the beautiful motion of colour through fog
the midnight moonstone blush
of an etiolated heart
what a soul-fade grey-weather sun
these bar-shadow silences
too long in the still
and songless humdrum hours of empty air
an unwound slowing
of slowness gone slower
like a held hand dying

all meaningful darkness
all stone-centred secrets
all depths below light
have one plunge
in the gather of hope
and I've a small sky
that I carry
a battering blue
from the luminous blindness of dream.

This Hand — 2008

Hotel Tropicoco

I love my dear old Russian lady
gone to seed
set like a ship that's run aground along the road
below a hill beside the sea
the water in her pool
goes briefly green
her rain-soaked roof
is leaking like a canopy of tropic trees
her paint is scaling
and her floors lie cracked
no revelers, nor teachers drunk with spring
are here
no
what force of soul she feels
is in the sand and wind
and warm aromas
of a wave-worn coast
an old man sweeps his cane
and sets a box seat
in the weeds
to watch us walking
to and from the beach
"hola, amigo," I say
he says the same
my pulse leaps like a beetle
from a strand of grass
the light receives my life

The Mirrors of Eden

with Adam
the image of God
the red earth
gasped and woke
to the lonesome
predicament of paradise
and what he might
have seen
in the black pool
of his otherwise blind-water
companion
a night-sky moon
or some palm-slaked
sorrowing solitude
like a vanishing kiss
of a child's lost dream
on the cusp of a deeper exhale

and then
that sleep of bone
that theft of boat-shaped breath
when angels
came creaturing down
bewinged and smoothed closed
bereft as fruit
with no stone
or seedless as unsexed grass

and this otherness
aged into knowing

the wise-eyed sadness
of love

Listening

Listening to
mast-rope rhythms
in this high wind
on the north shore of Cuba
I wonder
whose is the madder music
this relentless island drummer
eratic and wild
on the world-breathed edge
of the sea
or the foam-curled combers
failing the sky as they crest and shatter and
fall and turn under
in turbulent yearning
to mark eternity
with a singular voice
and water-volumed rush and roar to be gone
like my life
my sand-piper spirit
my two-palmed sun-touched soul
my five-coined mind
my slow-handed heart
receive this dog thought

I am only but briefly here
in this poem

in the rhythm of these words said aloud
in the steel-slapped midst
of this wonderful wind-driven world

Hemingway's Mirror

by way of jest
at Hemingway's house
Finca La Vigia in Cuba
near the fishing village of Cojimar
I say, 'see how he has
    my photograph
        hanging on his bathroom wall'
and there I am
my image in the mirror
above the vanity
where he must also
have seen himself
in the metaphysics of morning
as it is
with most men
waking to shave
or trim the aging mask
we wear
the flesh and bone
and ragged hair
of individual man …

I almost glimpse
the movement of
a whiskered mouth
or hear
the snipping
of a tufted ear
or catch a vapoured whiff

of sleeper's breath
befogged by silence
and a wisp of eidelon's amazed regret

I live in ink pots only
and my quill is dry
and stiff
as overwaxing
in a black moustache

the laughter
that you hear
is yours and mine

I join the sages
in the vacant silver
of a vanishing glance

There Is a Story

there is a story
suggesting that when
the great American beauty
Ava Gardner
swam naked in Hemingway's pool
and Earnest's wife
caught wind of him watching
from the vantage of his second writing room
training his telescope
on the lovely body
of the unclothed starlet
lapping her blue-washed lengths
the writer's partner
in a jealous pique
slipped down the walk
and stole her rival's robes
like Hera punishing Zeus by way of his women

and Ava was thereby forced
to return to the main house
like a naked child
save the black isosolese
of her pudendum
and the crimson O
of her full-breasted areola
crushed beneath her angry arms

and she
was Sheba-proud
in the full flush of their guestly gaze

and all the milk-fed gentlemen
were quick
with courtly shade
as stories go of gods and goddesses
at play

This Is How I Know—a Cuban Valentine

February 14th, 2008

this is how I know I love you
that day
you took a pratfall
on the serious banana
of a slippery floor
and cracked your head
on hard marble
in the ankle-deep rainwater
of hotel Tropicoco Cuba
and the day maid
came and found me
talking to a tourist from Penticton
and she told me
"su esposa, esta en
l'infirmaria"
as she gestured with her
hand flat-shadowed to the floor
so I followed and I found you
your hair wet
as a crushed mango
and you smiled through tears
and said *I'm sorry*

the doctor came in
angry to the knees
and waspish having waded
in through roadwash
he cut away the gory tresses
tonsured you
for stitches
afixed a little white hat
of folded gauze
and when I called you
my little Hutterite
you laughed
when I said
it looked like an airline pillow
stuck there
and told you to stop using
so much hair gel
you smiled

when I mentioned
that you looked like a novice Franciscan
you did not flinch
or snap
como una vieja like an old one
I said to the nurse
and she laughed
a sad regretful rica
despite her brave concern
una vieja I'd said
seeking the word for bald

and when we went to bed
I lay awake
watching you breathe
seeing the gentle
rise and fall of the counterpane
like the tired rhythms of a quiet sea

thinking—this is how I know
I love you
because my world
would turn to stone
without you

The Informer

"this is where the informer
lived"
a friendly Cuban fellow says
of a house in Havana
"when I was
an adolescent
the Beatles were forbidden here
and I had
a single record
which we played in secret
at my home.
One day this person
heard a joyful noise
and suddenly
we were surrounded
by police
who came to confiscate
my music"

'You were listening
to forbidden American songs,'
he said—
I told him 'No! —
this group is English—'

'Never mind that!' he said
'You are in serious trouble!'
he said.
'Surrender the record

and come with me!'
he said.

'No, my brother—' I replied.
'You are young like me.
Just listen
and decide.'

"I played
the song and he
smiled to hear
the brilliance of the band."

'I'm sorry,' he said.
'Be careful,' he said.

the informer
is a shadow
on the street

and as we parted
he and I
our hearts were light with life

"this was the house
of the informer"

he said
"I don't know
 where he's gone …"

The Wind is Like a Thief

the wind is like a thief
it steals my money
with its breath
and I must chase it
like a child
a paper moth

last night
a key-latch insect
fluttered from my startled hand
it clung
to the escutcheon
till I came
then flew
to thrill my heart
with fear of living silk
and lit and danced
two damaged wings
and left its dusty flight
upon the floor

my mind
a smudge-path of its going
like the sadness of a troubled thought
the grief of loss
seed-shadowed
where it struck

and so
I run to tramp
the single sorrow
of my money briefly free

I capture
in my footprint
with my cruel and steady shoe
what might purchase me
ten coins to hold
the morning
in a single servant's smile

Mistakes Along the Way

for Tai Grove

"What mistakes have you made along the way?"
he askes
meaning—how did you
arrive at this
new poem ...

and I think
I write as a river
flowing within the fluvial
absence of rain
I am as
summer in the shallows
with one mudcat
gasping in the marl
marking its way in the loblolly
like the self-shaping sprue of a mould

oh earth
oh waterless spawn
oh lovely fardel of true death
what suspires
like the pleasure of women
is here
in this fanning for breath

this sad convulsion of a last unlasting desire
where darkness dims down
to the silting of brown

what bends
and stones
and burbles at my broken voice
where heaven shatters into foam
or blinds the sun
with shade
or black refuses blue inclusions
of a fragrant fallen sky
upfloating
both the green illusion
of the willow and the larch
and the lost-leaf ant boats
of a leaf-rich branch

with each mistake
each mutable incantation
of a stolen clod
or pebble-thrill
where water frills
in radiant waves

small in amplitude and radius and reach
I fail
as I fail here
to be the thing I name
but what a lovely chaos
to be thus accused
and what
a final silence
fore and aft
I'm watering away
in errors all along
to touch
the flood of dawn
as darkness touches light

The Lost Girl

enflesh these disarticulated bones
this lost girl
curled to sleep away
six centuries of subterranean stone
within the water hollows of the earth
she sought and found the luminous darkness
dying young
and now she rests
like windless sticks
beneath as sad sarcophagus
she lies uncaved, the limestone rivers
of life-seeking seas
regret their work and weep
to fang an overarching malachite
or thrust green teeth
upon the jawline of a sharpened floor

hang back her heart
that winter fruit
old women cross their venous hands
to hold
and feel again that wizened thrum
of love's first call
the dancer's rose
the bloom of sugar
stained

the cherry in a tree of songs
such hungers
in the winds of spring
suspend the rhythms
in our water's time
like joyful foreheads bobbing in the sea

this girl
who, were she here
might ask her father
for a dress of age
might feel
the full circumference of feminary life
as it awakes and lights its lantern
in the womb
to show
how fertile circles sometimes seed
the earth

but she
was driven deep by fear
she fled
metallic monsters
from the traveler's tide
those emissaries of a greedy Queen
the slaughtering few
who cut the waves for gold

oh in the bone bowl
of her skull
dry water shows me what she was

the hollow marrow has my ink
I've tongueless words
and breathless black
and ears
against the stone

This is What I Know of God

for Kim Grove

I sat and watched
a sand crab
in my footprint
by the sea.

And as I watched
the sand crab
I saw him
watching me.

The Coat Within the Man

what can you tell
from the careless folds
of a good man's coat

is this the rumpled linen
of the soul

who wears this empty-shouldered slump
or fills this sleeve
like wind in wings
is there
within the redolent weave
from hollow cuff
and worn lapel
four buttons tug
the truth in us
to prove
a lag of thread
an elbow
smoothed by thought

the tailor rocks his eye
to feed the loom
and flax fields sway
with cloud-lit sweeps of ever-changing shade

Real Shoes

for Marty

"I see you've finally bought yourself
a pair of real shoes,"
he says
coming to that cobbler's conclusion
by quality of shine

and yes, my friend
I sank walking with you
in muck
crossing a boggy field
in France
and I wore that stench
for months

and he smiles
as he remembers
how we'd gone together
and purchased a pair each
of ten-dollar blue-canvas deck shoes
that felt on our feet
like frugal perfection

and I think, as I'm thinking
of the shoes of my life I'm thinking of

how my father wore expensive Dacks
and old-man's Hart and
Kodiaks with the bear fierce on the box
that smelled of new leather
and his father, my grandfather
wore black-felt hightops
and the hired man
wore only rubber
all year long
so at the end of his life
it was from blisters
failing to heal
that he vanished into empty hollows of vacant boots

and I'm fond to recall
the well-tooled cowboy boots
I wore as a boy
till the heels were gone
in the grass
or the Beatle boots I purchased
in Detroit in '65
that made me almost
cool as I clicked along halls at school
like the slow and steady come along of horses

or the pigskin desert boots
those rain-ruined
velvet-leathered things
that turned brittle
when they'd been wet only once

and I thought of my Berks-and-socks phase
of my purple Doc Martins
of my boyhood PF-flyer dreams ...

And I thought of how
in the hill trails of Cuba
a barefoot boy sat down in the dirt
and failed to find
a shoe that fit
amongst the runners we'd brought
to give away

and he wept
though he was twelve
he sobbed in the green scraps
and the fallen fronds
of the Royal palms
he grieved as he shook from shoulder to sole
to go away

shoeless

This Hand

for Manuel

I offer you
this hand, my friend
though I be armless here
as ancient garden stone, yet still
I hold
to open blue
the lifeline of my cloud-thinned palm
as sparrow-hearted
as the hungry song of winter seed at home
a singing spirit of such feathered truth
what morning says
to waking houses
when all the sorrowful music
of a troubled world
is heard
within a single sob
I thrill the distance
as the nearly drowned might grip
a strand of light from water sky
I see there's still
such helpless hope in this
the sad belief
in love
in all is everything
and moonlight
says one name, one name
one name upon the fragrant fulmination
in the dying combers
of a human sea

Notes on the poems:

In the School Rooms of Cuba: we visited a classroom in a mountain hamlet walking distance from our resort Marea del Portillo. It is well known that Cuba values education and that it has one of the highest literacy rates in the world. However, the year we visited the students were without books and they wrote with chalk on slate rather than using paper which is at a premium on the island

There Are Twisters on the Northern Beaches: while staying at Marea Del Portillo we witnessed a twister touch down and lift several times in the mountains.

To Drink the Earth on the Far Shore with Thirsty Feet: we brought shoes to give away and were very saddened by one young lad who could not find a pair of shoes to fit him. He sat and wept beside us on a mountain trail. Even some of the construction workers in the local construction site went barefoot.

Sealing the Jar: in Holguin Museum of Man there is a display of the various stages in the development of the human fetus.

Remembering the October Missile Crisis: it was fascinating to hear this event as seen from the point of view of our Cuban friends who like us were children at the time.

Charo De Maita: is a pre-Columbian/post-contact excavation site where the graves of indigenous Cuban

Indians are on display in glass covered sarcophagus.
The Drought: 2006 was a year of terrible drought for the island of Cuba.

Flowers of Fire: near Holguin there is a statue commemorating the arrival of Columbus.

Bad Water: in 2007 I was stung by a jellyfish called a Portuguese man-of-war which in Spanish is known as 'agua mala—bad water.'

The Lonesome Lovebird: in the lobby of Hotel Tropicoco there are birds in cages. One cage contains a single lovebird. Apparently, lovebirds, contrary to their name, are very aggressive and inclined to peck one another if they are kept in the same cage.

The Lost Girl: inspired by the skeleton of an indigenous teen found in a cave in Cuba

This is What I Know of God: one day while walking Kim Grove and I were talking about the fact that she has difficulty writing about God. That morning, I sat on the beach and watched a hermit crab watching me. I wrote this poem to demonstrate what I'd meant when in trying to help Kim, I quoted Emily Dickinson's line, 'say it slant.'

This Hand: Manuel Leon often closes his e mails by way of friendship with the phrase—this hand—which has come to represent our fellowship and the spirit of good feelings arising from our cultural exchanges as Canadian poets among Cuban friends.

Biographical Sketch of Author

In 2005 John B. Lee was inducted as Poet Laureate of Brantford in perpetuity. The same year he received the distinction of being named Honourary Life Member of The Canadian Poetry Association. In 2007 he was made a member of the Chancellor's Circle of the President's Club of McMaster University and named first recipient of the Souwesto Award for his contribution to literature in his home region of southwestern Ontario. A recipient of over sixty prestigious international awards for his writing he is winner of the $10,000 CBC Literary Award for Poetry, the only two-time recipient of the People's Poetry Award, and 2006 winner of the inaugural Souwesto Orison Writing Award (University of Windsor).

In 2007 he was named winner of the Winston Collins Award for Best Canadian Poem. He has well-over fifty books published to date and is the editor of seven anthologies including two best-selling works: That Sign of Perfection: poems and stories on the game of hockey; and Smaller Than God: words of spiritual longing. His work has appeared internationally in over 500 publications, and has been translated into French, Spanish, Korean and Chinese. He has read his work in nations all over the world including South Africa, France, Korea, Cuba, Canada and the United States. He has received letters of praise from Nelson Mandela, Desmond Tutu, Australian Poet, Les Murray, and Senator Romeo Dallaire. Called "the greatest living poet in English," by poet George Whipple, he lives in Port Dover, Ontario where he works as a full-time author.

Previouisly published by
Hidden Brook Press
www.HiddenBrookPress.com

In the Muddy Shoes of Morning
ISBN 978-1-897475-64-5

Sweet Cuba
The Building of a Poetic Tradition: 1608-1958
Translators: John B. Lee, Dr. Manuel de Jesús Velázquez León
ISBN 978-1-897475-53-9

www.ingramcontent.com/pod-product-compliance
Lightning Source LLC
Chambersburg PA
CBHW021122080526
44587CB00010B/601